30-Day Journey

with Dorothy Day

30-Day Journey

with Dorothy Day

Compiled and Edited by Coleman Fannin

Fortress Press
Minneapolis

30-DAY JOURNEY WITH DOROTHY DAY

Cover design: Paul Soupiset
Interior design: Paul Soupiset
Typesetting: Jessica Ess, Hillspring Books

Print ISBN: 978-1-5064-5107-7
eBook ISBN: 978-1-5064-5108-4

The paper used in this publication meets the minimum requirements of American National Standard for Information Sciences — Permanence of Paper for Printed Library Materials, ANSI Z329.48-1984.

Manufactured in the U.S.A.

Contents

Introduction vii

Days 1-30 1

Further Reading 63

The greatest challenge of the day is: how to bring about a revolution of the heart, a revolution which has to start with each one of us? When we begin to take the lowest place, to wash the feet of others, to love our brothers with that burning love, that passion, which led to the Cross, then we can truly say, "Now I have begun."

Day after day we accept our failure, but we accept it because of our knowledge of the victory of the Cross.

—Dorothy Day, *Loaves and Fishes*

Introduction

Despite reportedly having said, "Don't call me a saint," Dorothy Day may soon be declared one. Day was an American journalist and social activist who converted to Catholicism at the age of thirty. Together with Peter Maurin, she started the *Catholic Worker* newspaper in 1933, inspiring a movement of independent "houses of hospitality," where Catholic Workers still live in community, serve the poor, and resist war and injustice today. Day wrote numerous books and articles and edited the paper for nearly fifty years, and the cause for her canonization has been approved by the United States Conference of Catholic Bishops.

Day was born in Brooklyn on November 8, 1897, the third of five children, but spent most of her childhood in Chicago. Although her parents were nominal Christians, she prayed and read the Bible on her own and was baptized and confirmed in the Episcopal Church at thirteen. In high school, however, she abandoned her faith as she became increasingly aware of social problems. She joined the Socialist Party and wrote columns and short stories while a student at the University of Illinois, only to drop out and move back to New York City with her family. There she worked for Socialist periodicals, reporting on meetings and protests by labor unions and other radical groups but rarely participating in them. Meanwhile, she befriended writers and activists and had a number of affairs, as well as a brief marriage. She subsequently lived in Chicago and New Orleans before purchasing a cottage on Staten Island in 1924 with the proceeds from selling the movie rights to a recently published novel.

Day spent the next few years in a live-in relationship with Forster Batterham, an anarchist and atheist with whom she found what she called "natural happiness." This happiness revived her religious sense, and she began to pray more and go to Mass. Her faith and an unexpected pregnancy caused conflict with Batterham, which increased after she had their daughter baptized, but she hesitated before separating from him and joining the Catholic Church in late 1927.

Although Day regarded the Catholic Church as "the church of the poor," she thought it offered the poor only charity, and for a time she continued to work for an affiliate of the Communist Party. She did not know many Catholics, apart from a few priests, and the Great Depression left her feeling disconnected from other radicals. Still, she focused on her spiritual life and began to write for Catholic publications. In 1932, *Commonweal* assigned her to cover a hunger march in Washington, DC, after which she prayed that "some way would open up for me to use what talents I possessed for my fellow workers, for the poor." Later in

Manhattan, where she was living at the time, Day met self-described peasant Peter Maurin, who was looking to popularize his ideas. Born in 1877, he had been involved with Catholic groups in France, then had worked as a laborer and teacher around Canada and the United States. In addition to embracing voluntary poverty, he had studied personalist philosophy and Catholic social teaching and found a vision of "building a new society within the shell of the old." To this end, he had devised a program consisting of regular meetings for discussion or "clarification of thought," houses for performing works of mercy (practices that meet the material and spiritual needs of others), and communes for farming the land.

Maurin provided Day with the Catholic education she lacked and the opportunity for which she had prayed; she broadened his vision while crediting him with founding the Catholic Worker movement. It was she who insisted on naming the newspaper after the Communist *Daily Worker*. The first issue of the *Catholic Worker* was printed on May 1, 1933, and sold on the streets for a penny a copy. Its circulation grew to a hundred thousand within a year and nearly twice that within five years. Its office in Day's apartment also attracted people in need of food, clothing, and shelter, along with donations and volunteers, which necessitated renting a house; similar houses soon appeared in other cities. Eventually, the community bought its first farm outside the city. Members engaged in direct action in support of higher wages and better working conditions.

The initial success of the movement was short-lived, however, as Day faced criticism for her pacifist stand during the Spanish Civil War and World War II. Wartime also meant that subscriptions plummeted and most of the houses closed. Then Maurin died in 1949. Nevertheless, the Catholic Workers rebounded in the Cold War era, and Day was renewed by becoming a Benedictine oblate (a person who affiliates with a monastic community but does not take full monastic vows) and regularly taking intense spiritual retreats. In the 1950s she was arrested several times for refusing to take part in civil defense drills. In the 1960s she twice went to Rome to advocate for the Second Vatican Council to condemn modern warfare and support conscientious objection. Catholic Workers were also active in the civil rights movement and the opposition to the Vietnam War. In addition to writing, Day traveled around the country speaking to Catholic Worker communities and joining their efforts. Although she experienced tension with the hierarchy, she remained a faithful Catholic who attended daily Mass, studied the Bible and the lives of the saints, and affirmed the doctrines of the church until her death on November 29, 1980.

The passages in this book provide a window into the spiritual life that shaped and sustained Day's commitments to nonviolence and economic justice. Although she possessed these commitments prior to her conversion, she came to ground them in Scripture and tradition and indeed to demonstrate the compatibility of orthodox Christian belief and radical social action. Her intent was "to blow the dynamite of the church," as Maurin put it. She criticized capitalism and socialism alike for exploiting the masses to achieve the goals of the state and offered an alternative that centers on the human person and emphasizes community, private property, and economic cooperation. As you journey with her, you will discover a witness defined by discipleship, not ideology, and a spirit not only imbued with the love of God and neighbor but also marked by contemplation and introspection. May you find this witness transformative.

Days 1–30

It is hard to understand the love of God for us. We pray daily to increase in the love of God because we know that if we love a person very much, all things become easy to us and delightful. We want, rather unreasonably, sensible feelings of love. St. Teresa says that the only way we can measure the love we have for God is the love we have for our fellows. So by working for our fellows we come to love them. That you understand, for you believe that you are working for them when you give hours every morning to the distribution of literature, climbing tenement-house stairs, knocking at doors, suffering rebuffs, enduring heat and cold, weariness and hardships to bring to them what you consider a gospel which will set them free.

And if you and I love our faulty fellow-human beings, how much more must God love us all? If we as human parents can forgive our children any neglect, any crime, and work and pray patiently to make them better, how much more does God love us?

You may say perhaps: "How do we know He does, if there is a He!" And I can only answer that we know it because He is here present with us today in the Blessed Sacrament on the altar, that He never has left us, and that by daily going to Him for the gift of Himself as daily bread, I am convinced of that love. I have the Faith that feeding at that table has nourished my soul so that there is life in it, and a lively realization that there is such a thing as the love of Christ for us.

Reflection

Day says that we should not simply expect to have feelings of love for God but instead must *learn* to love God, specifically by learning to love "our faulty fellow-human beings" through working for their earthly good. This work leads her not to sadness over the things she has endured or sacrificed but to joy over the love she has received.

God's love is easy to invoke but hard to understand, and even harder to practice. But we can gain understanding through both action and contemplation. Here, Day reflects on the act of taking Communion and actively caring for the needs of others. By serving others, we can experience and share love. We are created in the image of God and meet God in each other.

Day's first autobiography was *From Union Square to Rome*, published in 1938. It captures her perspective after a decade as a Catholic, particularly her desire to engage the problems of the world within the context of the faith of the church.

As Day would do frequently over the years, she draws from the wisdom of the saints and points to the grace of the sacraments—in this case, Teresa of Ávila and the doctrine of the real presence, according to which the elements of bread and wine become the body and blood of Christ in their essence.

When the Apostles wanted to call down fire from heaven on the inhospitable Samaritans, the "enemies" of the Jews, Jesus said to them, "You know not of what Spirit you are." When Peter told Our Lord not to accept the way of the Cross and His own death, He said, "Get behind me, Satan. For you are not on the side of God but of men." But He also had said "Thou art Peter and upon this rock I will build my church." Peter denied Jesus three times at that time in history, but after the death on the Cross, and the Resurrection and the Descent of the Holy Spirit, Peter faced up to Church and State alike and said, "We must obey God rather than men." Deliver us, O Lord, from the fear of our enemies, which makes cowards of us all.

I can sit in the presence of the Blessed Sacrament and wrestle for that peace in the bitterness of my soul, a bitterness which many Catholics throughout the world feel, and I can find many things in Scripture to console me, to change my heart from hatred to love of enemy. "Our worst enemies are those of our own household," Jesus said.

Reflection

We all struggle to obey God rather than our own desires, and our negative feelings toward others—enemies or friends—are the source of many forms of violence. Thirty years after she wrote the previous passage, and in the midst of the Vietnam War, Day perceived that peace begins in individual hearts, which can only be transformed slowly and with God's help. Here, she asks for the grace to help overcome her bitterness and be obedient to God, something for which we all must ask, not least with respect to our relationships with individuals or communities. Who do you fear, or at least find hard to love? Consider how you can act with love toward those you fear or dislike (or even hate).

We must contain ourselves in patience, remembering each morning that our main job is to love God, and to serve Him and if we don't get things done due to interruptions, well, it cannot be helped, and God will take care of what we leave undone. But a tranquil spirit is important. St. Teresa says that God cannot rest in an unquiet heart. I have to remember that many times during the day.

What if everything goes to rack and ruin? We can only do what we can to make order, but in the long run it's ourselves we have to look after. So daily Mass, and *meditation*, and spiritual reading. What about an extra fifteen minutes after Mass? It will help and the house will not fall apart. You may be distracted, you may be in a frenzy about the work to do, you may want to get to the post office, but the very effort of will holding you there is a prayer.

Day corresponded with family and friends throughout her life, as well as with a number of public figures (including Cesar Chavez and Thomas Merton) and Catholic Workers in many cities after the movement began. This excerpt is from a 1940 letter to Joe Zarrella, who helped her manage the New York house of hospitality, in which she thanks him for "keeping things going" but counsels him to avoid becoming bogged down in planning and organizing the movement's activities.

Reflection

Even when it comes from an impulse to serve God and help others, the "unquietness" or restlessness of our hearts, as well as the stress of the many demands placed on us in our daily lives, can leave us perpetually dissatisfied and ungrateful. Patience may have been the most important virtue Day acquired after her conversion, and she constantly tried to impart it to her readers and fellow Catholic Workers. It is powerful and instructive to see someone who devoted so much of her time and energy to helping others observe that in the long run we must take care of ourselves. No matter how flawed our participation in spiritual practices, such as those Day mentions, they allow God to enter our hearts and allow us to find peace and better serve our neighbors. What tasks and distractions make your heart restless? What practices would help you develop patience?

Day Four

One of the professors who lectured us was pointing out how Utopias would never work. But always it is the ideal of a Utopia held up that has influenced the masses.

There is always a great need of idealists who hold up the ideal rather than the practical. Without them men would not strive so high. Little by little, it can be found that the ideal works and is practical and then people are surprised.

. . .

Christ said, "Be ye therefore perfect even as your Father in Heaven is perfect." "Go ye therefore and sell what you have and give to the poor." "If you have two coats take one and give it to your brother, and if your brother asks you for your coat, give him your cloak too."

People do not scoff at these words because they are the words of Christ. A great many regard them hopelessly and falling back on their poor humanity they admit their inability to live up to these words. But nevertheless these words (hard words) go down through the ages, and through them many have followed the precept as well as the counsel. And have influenced humanity greatly thereby.

This visit by a professor less than a year after the first issue of the newspaper indicates that the Catholic Workers were already implementing the first point in Peter Maurin's program: regular meetings for discussion or "clarification of thought." Likewise, Day was

Reflection

It is usually wise to be practical, but always focusing on what is immediately practical or sensible can limit what may be possible. Imagining an ideal can allow possibilities to emerge. Although the Catholic Workers were frequently criticized for being utopian, Day did not believe that most Christians would or could follow the Sermon on the Mount to the letter, at least not anytime soon. Rather, she was an idealist in that she believed we should strive for the very best whether or not success seems likely. We are called to witness to the ideal, not to wait for a majority to adopt it.

Without a vision that calls us beyond what we think is possible, we are more susceptible to quick fixes that do not address underlying problems, whereas with such a vision (and time and patience), we may find unexpected, and ultimately more effective, solutions. What ideals influence you? Imagine what it would be like to pursue them without restraint.

already emphasizing the Sermon on the Mount (the source of these words of Christ), which she would later call "our manifesto."

In Catholic theology, chastity, poverty, and obedience are counsels for those who want to become perfect (i.e., members of religious orders), not precepts that are binding for everyone.

Today we are not contented with little achievements, with small beginnings. We should look to St. Teresa, the Little Flower, to walk her little way, her way of love. We should look to St. Teresa of Avila who was not content to be like those people who proceeded with the pace of hens about God's business, but like those people who on their own account were greatly daring in what they wished to do for God. It is we ourselves that we have to think about, no one else. That is the way the saints worked. They paid attention to what they were doing and if others were attracted to them by their enterprise, why, well and good. But they looked to themselves first of all.

Do what comes to hand. Whatsoever thy hand finds to do, do it with all thy might. After all, God is with us. It shows too much conceit to trust to ourselves, to be discouraged at what we ourselves can accomplish. It is lacking in faith in God to be discouraged. After all, we are going to proceed with His help. We offer Him what we are going to do. If He wishes it to prosper, it will. We must depend solely on Him. Work as though everything depended on ourselves, and pray as though everything depended on God, as St. Ignatius says.

Reflection

Regardless of our motivations, wishing to do great things is dangerous, especially in a culture that celebrates grand (and efficient) achievements. It is hard to avoid either playing it safe, thereby squandering our gifts, or measuring success according to immediate and definite results, thereby tempting us to use less-than-admirable means. Day was daring in her work, but she also managed to focus more on being faithful than on achieving certain ends, however good, which kept her from becoming discouraged. This was undoubtedly because of her dedication to walking the little way of love, a dedication we would do well to share. Instead of worrying about your success today, rest in the value of the time, energy, and courage you devote to your work.

Day wrote two versions of the story of the Catholic Worker movement, the first being *House of Hospitality*, published in 1939. In this passage she mentions three saints: Ignatius of Loyola, the sixteenth-century founder of the Society of Jesus (the Jesuits); Teresa of Ávila, a sixteenth-century nun and the author of *The Interior Castle*, a spiritual classic; and Teresa (Thérèse) of Lisieux, a nineteenth-century nun who was popularly known as "the Little Flower of Jesus" and whose pursuit of holiness through small, everyday acts came to be known as the "little way," a source of inspiration for the Catholic Worker.

We all wish for recognition of one kind or another. But it is mass action people think of these days. They lose sight of the sacrament of the present moment—of the little way.

Like Lord Jim, in Conrad's story, we are all waiting for great opportunities to show heroism, letting countless opportunities go by to enlarge our hearts, increase our faith, and show our love for our fellows, and so for Him. As St. Paul says, it is by little and by little that we are saved—or that we fall. We are living in this world and must make choices now, choices which may mean the sacrifice of our lives, in the future, but for now our goods, our reputations even. Our work is called futile, our stand of little worth or significance, having no influence, winning no converts, ineffective if not a form of treason. Or it is termed defeatism, appeasement, escapism.

What a paradox it is, this natural life and this supernatural life. We must give up our lives to gain them; we must die to live; we must be pruned to bear fruit. Ah yes, when we are being called appeasers, defeatists, we are being deprived of our dearest goods—our reputation, honor, the esteem of men—and we are truly on the way to becoming the despised of the earth. We are beginning perhaps to be truly poor.

Reflection

God, and sometimes only God, sees what we choose and knows what we sacrifice, and this supernatural perspective is the one that ultimately matters. Here, Day discusses the divine significance of everyday acts in terms of "the sacrament of the present moment," by which she means a sign through which we receive grace.

As she knew from experience, other choices we make in our attempts to be faithful can result in scorn from others, especially when those choices challenge the status quo of the state or its economy. We must develop not only the discernment to know when and how to challenge the status quo but also the strength to endure losing "our dearest goods." Like Day's voluntary poverty, unpopularity can have the benefit of deepening our solidarity with all those who may be despised by people but are loved by God. What kinds of sacrifices have you made? Be encouraged and know that your hard choices are valuable, even when unrecognized.

Day contrasts the little way of St. Thérèse of Lisieux with the behavior of the protagonist in Joseph Conrad's novel *Lord Jim*. As a young man, Jim dreams of a life of adventure and becomes a sailor, but then, when presented with the opportunity to be a hero, he decides to abandon ship, seemingly condemning the other passengers to death. Although they survive, he is haunted by the memory of his decision.

When it is said that we disturb people too much by the words pacifism and anarchism, I can only think that people need to be disturbed, that their consciences need to be aroused, that they do indeed need to look into their work, and study new techniques of love and poverty and suffering for each other. Of course the remedies are drastic, but then too the evil is a terrible one and we are all involved, we are all guilty, and most certainly we are all going to suffer. The fact that we have "the faith," that we go to the sacraments, is not enough. "Inasmuch as ye have done it unto the least of these my brethren, ye have done it unto me" with napalm, nerve gas, our hydrogen bomb, our "new look."

Each one of us must make our decisions as to what he should do, each one must examine his conscience and beg God for strength.

Day's pacifism had a clear grounding in the teachings of Jesus, although that did not make it more popular. The nature of her anarchism is less concrete, but in practice it meant that she did not vote or pay income tax despite being deeply engaged in public affairs. In her youth she was inspired by Leo Tolstoy, who based his own anarchism and pacifism on the teachings of Jesus. Peter Maurin introduced her to the thought of Russian anarchist Peter Kropotkin.

Reflection

The notion that we need to be disturbed can be challenging and upsetting, especially when we are comfortable with our lives as they are. Encountering new ideas, such as the idea that pacifism or anarchism could be compatible with the Christian faith, can give us pause and open our minds to different approaches.

For Day, being willing to look at the world differently and to live in a manner that takes all people into account is not merely an admirable supplement to her faith; it is an essential part of it. Everyone is affected by warfare, for example, but the poor bear the brunt of it. We must examine our consciences not only in light of various ideas and beliefs but also in conversation with God. Begin by opening your mind to new and challenging ideas.

The "new look" mentioned here was the national security policy of the Eisenhower administration, a policy associated with the military strategy of massive retaliation directed at the Soviet Union.

One of the greatest evils of the day among those outside of prison is the sense of futility. Young people say, What good can one person do? What is the sense of our small effort? They cannot see that we must lay one brick at a time, take one step at a time; we can be responsible only for the one action of the present moment. But we can beg for an increase of love in our hearts that will vitalize and transform all our individual actions, and know that God will take them and multiply them, as Jesus multiplied the loaves and fishes.

Published in 1963, *Loaves and Fishes* is Day's second account of the Catholic Worker movement (after *House of Hospitality*). Her biography of St. Thérèse of Lisieux, titled simply *Thérèse*, was published three years earlier, and prior to this passage she discusses the saint's little way in relation to a brief stay in jail after a protest. Day had read Thérèse's autobiography shortly after converting and found it tiresome, but her experience at a house of hospitality led her to appreciate the importance of personal responsibility and the power of seemingly insignificant acts.

Reflection

Most of us, young or not, can sympathize with feeling discouraged and useless at times, but Day emphasizes both acting in the moment and acquiring the capacity to act over time, notably through prayer. Although we can and should always take steps forward, an essential step is to call on God to help us take better actions and to trust God to make the actions we take more valuable.

The miracle (or miracles) of the feeding of the multitude, reported in all four Gospels, indicates that God not only sees our "small effort" but also builds on it. Sometimes God multiplies our actions in ways that are readily apparent; sometimes our goals are accomplished slowly and incrementally, if at all. It is therefore crucial for us to move forward and trust God if we are to sustain the kind of effort that leads to valuable change. Our external life is inseparable from our internal life, and every moment of our daily work requires faithfulness inside and out.

Day Nine

So often one is overcome with a tragic sense of the meaninglessness of our lives—patience, patience, and the very word means suffering. Endurance, perseverance, sacrament of the present moment, the sacrament of duty. One must keep on reassuring oneself of these things. And repeat acts of faith. "Lord, I believe, help thou my unbelief." We are placed here; why? To know Him, and so love Him, serve Him, by serving others and so attain to eternal life and joy, understanding, etc.

So it means study, and St. Thomas said the more we learned of the life around us the more we studied, the more we knew of God thru his creation. So—read, study, write, especially since by writing one is aiding others. When I write "I," the other reads "I." We each of us are unique, yet so alike too.

Day kept diaries for much of her life, mixing reports of ordinary events with thoughts on theology, literature, world affairs, and more. Some of her entries were published in the *Catholic Worker*, but others were private, and a selection of the latter was published in 2008.

This entry was written in June 1963, the same year the previous passage was published. Day had recently

Reflection

We are all susceptible to feelings of meaninglessness at some time or another, and Day's reflection reveals that she was no exception. However, she stresses patience and the little way or, as she terms it here, "the sacrament of duty." Day sees study and writing as central to the duty or vocation to which she is called, and it is her way of convincing herself and us that we are not alone. The more we seek to know God and serve others, the more we experience suffering in the sense she describes, but this shows us how much we need God. To both believe and not believe is part of the human condition, but this condition is not hopeless or without assurance, because we can know and love God (and be known and loved by God) through acts of faith. As your act of faith, find a new way to think and reflect, whether by reading a new book, learning something new, or writing in a journal.

returned from Rome, where she had joined a group of fifty women in urging Pope John XXIII to oppose the methods of modern warfare, only for him to succumb to cancer shortly thereafter.

"Lord, I believe, help thou my unbelief" references Mark 9:24.

Day Ten

Going to confession is hard. Writing a book is hard, because you are "giving yourself away." But if you love, you want to give yourself. You write as you are impelled to write, about man and his problems, his relation to God and his fellows. You write about yourself because in the long run all man's problems are the same, his human needs of sustenance and love. "What is man that Thou art mindful of him?" the Psalmist asks, and he indicates man's immense dignity when he says, "Thou hast made him a little less than the angels." He is made in the image and likeness of God, he is a temple of the Holy Spirit. He is of tremendous importance. What is man, where is he going, what is his destiny? It is a mystery. We are sons of God, and "it is a terrible thing to fall into the hands of the living God."

I can write only of myself, what I know of myself, and I pray with St. Augustine, "Lord, that I may know myself, in order to know Thee."

Day begins her second autobiography, *The Long Loneliness*, by describing going to confession, which she compares to writing about oneself. Even if she did not mention St. Augustine of Hippo, the allusion to his *Confessions* (widely considered the first autobiography) would be apparent. Her life had several parallels to his, not least her youthful love affairs and her desire to use her talents for others.

Reflection

Acknowledging our problems, and especially our failures, is hard. Being vulnerable is an important part of knowing ourselves and knowing God, but it can feel, as Day writes, like "a terrible thing." However, it is also a wonderful thing, because in becoming aware of our problems, we also become aware of our common humanity and our shared desires for love and acceptance. In seeking to know herself, Day discovered the need for illumination from God, who creates and sustains us and knows us better than we know ourselves. Day's awareness of the dignity and importance of every person compelled her to dedicate her life to serving the poor and opposing the violence that harms those made in the image and likeness of God. She saw weekly confession as vital to her life, and we must come to see an attitude of confession, of giving ourselves away, as vital to knowing God and ourselves. Do you regularly confess your struggles and failures to God? Reflect on the ways in which your confession might compel you to love those around you.

Augustine likely had in mind the aphorism "know thyself," famously inscribed on the Temple of Apollo at Delphi, the seat of the most important oracle of ancient Greece.

The greatest challenge of the day is: how to bring about a revolution of the heart, a revolution which has to start with each one of us? When we begin to take the lowest place, to wash the feet of others, to love our brothers with that burning love, that passion, which led to the Cross, then we can truly say, "Now I have begun."

Day after day we accept our failure, but we accept it because of our knowledge of the victory of the Cross.

Reflection

Patience is a virtue, but patience is not easy, particularly when we want to accomplish something good. Near the end of *Loaves and Fishes*, Day revisits themes of personal transformation, service to others, and trust in divine providence. She presents the cross as the ultimate example of the reality that our failure, genuine or only apparent, does not preclude success in the long run, because success is in God's hands.

Day uses the idea of "a revolution of the heart" to contrast the personalist philosophy of the Catholic Worker with the philosophies behind the communist and socialist revolutions of the mid-twentieth century, not to mention the philosophies behind capitalism. Every social system necessarily involves social sin, and only insofar as each one of us comes to repent and serve others will we truly change the world for the better. In the meantime, our task is to keep going, "day after day" (the title of Day's newspaper column in the 1930s and early 1940s), in loving those around us. What prevents you from fulfilling this task? How could you begin to take the lowest place?

Love and ever more love is the only solution to every problem that comes up. If we love each other enough, we will bear with each other's faults and burdens. If we love enough, we are going to light that fire in the hearts of others. And it is love that will burn out the sins and hatreds that sadden us. It is love that will make us want to do great things for each other. No sacrifice and no suffering will then seem too much.

Reflection

At first glance, the notion that love is "the only solution to every problem" may appear naïve or simplistic, and not only because Day was writing near the outset of World War II. The word *love* always sounds wonderful, but it is used so widely and indiscriminately that it can be almost meaningless. As she notes just prior to this passage, love can also be filled with "self-seeking," which is not an easy thing to realize or admit.

Love is wonderful, and it does solve problems, but only when given form and content. Day learned about love through the practice of spiritual disciplines, which reminded her of the sacrifice and suffering of Christ, and through daily life at a Catholic Worker house, which involved bearing with the faults and burdens of all sorts of people. Bearing with each other can be exhausting, but it can also become habitual and lead to greater love for each other. It is then that we are able to do "great things" for each other not merely out of duty but out of love. Think of something you would be willing to sacrifice and suffer out of love.

Day Thirteen

Whenever I groan within myself and think how hard it is to keep writing about love in these times of tension and strife, which may at any moment become for us all a time of terror, I think to myself, "What else is the world interested in?" What else do we all want, each one of us, except to love and be loved, in our families, in our work, in all our relationships? God is Love. Love casts out fear. Even the most ardent revolutionist, seeking to change the world, to overturn the tables of the money changers, is trying to make a world where it is easier for people to love, to stand in that relationship to each other. We want with all our hearts to love, to be loved. And not just in the family but to look upon all as our mothers, sisters, brothers, children. It is when we love the most intensely and most humanly that we can recognize how tepid is our love for others. The keenness and intensity of love brings with it suffering, of course, but joy too, because it is a foretaste of heaven. . . .

When you love people, you see all the good in them, all the Christ in them. God sees Christ, His Son, in us and loves us. And so we should see Christ in others, *and nothing else*, and love them. There can never be enough of it. There can never be enough thinking about it. St. John of the Cross said that where there was no love, put love and you would take out love. The principle certainly works.

Reflection

Our desires take many forms, but fundamentally each of us wants "to love and be loved," an idea with a long history in the Christian tradition. God is love and creates us to love, specifically to love God and, through God, other people. However, God also gives us the freedom to misdirect our love, which can leave us frustrated. Yet our longing remains.

Day's experience with communism meant that she understood something of the attitude of the revolutionary, which enabled her to look past disagreements to our common humanity without minimizing the importance of those disagreements. When we see all people as created in the image of God, we can develop greater understanding of and love for them, which, if nothing else, should motivate us to make a world where it is easier for all of us to love. Is there an absence of love anywhere in your life? How could you put more love into those areas?

On Pilgrimage was adapted from Day's diary entries during 1948, which also served as her regular column in the *Catholic Worker* that year. The format allows her to take stock of the Catholic Worker movement and the ideas that had come to define it over its first fifteen years.

In this passage she mentions St. John of the Cross, a friar and follower of St. Teresa of Ávila.

War is deviltry. It calls for sacrifices indeed, but not at the altar of love. "Greater love hath no man than this." A great blasphemy this, to use Christ's words in connection with men going to war. They go because they are drafted, because they are afraid of what their neighbors will say, because the pay is good, because the benefits accruing afterward (the G.I. Bill of Rights) are great. And they are told by press and pulpit that they are going because they love their fellows, and they are filled with a warm glow of self-love. And then they are given their intensive training in how to escape death, how to kill.

Greater love hath no man than this, that he lay down his life for his brothers, and the Russians are our brothers, the Negro is our brother, the Japanese are our brothers, the Germans, the Mexicans, the Filipinos, the Jews, the Arabs.

. . . We have not yet paid the price of peace, given up the friendship, love, esteem of the world. The folly of the cross. We do not yet know what it means. Loving our enemy. We only fear him. We have great possessions, like the young man in the Gospel, and we turn from Christ to the use of force to protect them. Not our Church, our school, our home.

Reflection

In wartime we may have trouble coping with the suffering caused or endured by soldiers, on our side or the other, let alone by civilians. Unfortunately, we often keep this suffering at a distance and comfort ourselves with patriotism and our "great possessions." We must be willing to lay down our lives for *some* things, so the question is *what* things. Our willingness to kill (or support those who kill) some people we do not know in order to protect other people we do know, not to mention our possessions or way of life, presents us with a dilemma in light of Christ's words about nonviolence and human dignity. Instead, Day suggests we should be willing to make sacrifices for peace, friendship, and loving even our enemies. Who do you have trouble treating as brothers or sisters? What might you be willing to give up for the sake of peace and friendship?

Day met Peter Maurin after returning from an assignment for *The Commonweal* (later simply *Commonweal*), a prominent Catholic journal to which she continued to contribute articles into the 1970s. However, this excerpt is from a letter to the editor in 1948, a letter to which managing editor C. G. Paulding appended a note of criticism.

"Greater love hath no man than this" references John 15:13, and "the folly of the cross" references 1 Corinthians 1:18.

His were hard sayings, so that even His own followers did not know what He was saying, did not understand Him. It was not until after He died on the Cross, it was not until He had suffered utter defeat, it would seem, and they thought their cause was lost entirely; it was not until they had persevered and prayed with all the fervor and desperation of their poor loving hearts, that they were enlightened by the Holy Spirit, and knew the truth with a strength that enabled them to suffer defeat and martyrdom in their turn. They knew then that not by force of arms, by the bullet or the ballot, would they conquer. They knew and were ready to suffer defeat—to show that great love which enabled them to lay down their lives for their friends.

And now the whole world is turning to "force" to conquer. Fascist and Communist alike believe that only by the shedding of blood can they achieve victory. Catholics, too, believe that suffering and the shedding of blood "must needs be," as Our Lord said to the disciples at Emmaus. But their teaching, their hard saying, is that they must be willing to shed every drop of their own blood, and not take the blood of their brothers. They are willing to die for their faith, believing that the blood of martyrs is the seed of the Church.

Reflection

Jesus's sayings are no less difficult for us to accept than they were for the disciples. Yet the disciples did accept the teaching to lay down their lives for their friends (John 15:13) and so did the early Christian martyrs whose deaths became "the seed of the Church." Here, Day challenges groups on all sides of armed conflicts. It is not simply that we turn to force at some point; we tend to do so even before we exhaust other avenues, which may be related to our unwillingness to suffer defeat. That is, we are more concerned with winning or "conquering" than with doing what is right. If we are to know a different way, then we must be willing to act with love and peace, even if it means losing. Day talks about war, but this challenge exists in our everyday lives. Consider small ways that you can choose doing what is right over what is advantageous.

Day Sixteen

Today the whole world is in the midst of a revolution. We are living through it now—all of us. History will record this time as a time of world revolution. And frankly, we are calling for Saints. The Holy Father in his call for Catholic Action, for the lay apostolate, is calling for Saints. We must prepare now for martyrdom—otherwise we will not be ready. Who of us if he were attacked now would not react quickly and humanly against such attack? Would we love our brother who strikes us? Of all at *The Catholic Worker* how many would not instinctively defend himself with any forceful means in his power? We must prepare. We must prepare now. There must be a disarmament of the heart.

With the outbreak of the Spanish Civil War in 1936, more and more readers objected to Day's pacifism. She declined to support either the church hierarchy, which sided with the largely Catholic rebels (the Nationalists), or the anarchists and communists allied with the established government (the Republicans). Prior to this passage, however, she notes the martyrdom of priests and nuns by Republican forces, and after it she mentions Hitler and Mussolini.

Catholic Action is a movement of loosely related lay organizations that share the goal of transforming society. It was most fully developed by Pope Pius XI, the "Holy Father" to whom Day refers.

Reflection

Although the disarmament of governments or factions seems to be out of reach, "a disarmament of the heart" is a possibility for every one of us. To be sure, Day and her readers were not in immediate danger of being attacked, and neither are we. Nevertheless, as terrible as it is to imagine the possibility of being attacked, we must prepare now if we hope to respond out of love rather than the instinct for self-preservation. Life provides us with many opportunities to pursue peace and reconciliation, but we can also prepare by being honest about the internal sources of conflict: our envy of and anger toward others, our desire for power and control, and so on. Ask God to search your heart for these things, trusting that God will guide you toward right action.

"All the way to heaven is heaven, because Christ said, 'I am the Way.'" And work should be part of heaven, not part of hell. In the black underground caverns where the miners lose all light of day—month after month, from early fall till late spring—there is a glimpse of "everlasting night where no order is and everlasting horror dwelleth." We want to change man's work; we want to make people question their work; is it on the way to heaven or hell?

Man gains his bread by his work. It is his bread and wine. It is his life. We cannot emphasize the importance of it enough. We must emphasize the holiness of *work*, and we must emphasize the sacramental quality of *property*, too. That means the property of the poor. They have very little of it. We know that it is dangerous, it corrupts, it is almost a testing ground in this life of attachment and detachment. We must love it as a sample of God's providence and goodness and we must be ready to give it up.

As part of a series of columns on the theme of work, Day discusses a visit to western Pennsylvania, where she spoke with a number of striking coal miners and their families; the strikes were led by the well-known union president John L. Lewis and drew national attention.

The first quote in this passage (one of Day's favorites) is from St. Catherine of Siena, a fourteenth-century nun and theologian; the second is from Job 10:22.

Reflection

Our work affects the course of our lives, and we devote significant time to doing it, but we do not always reflect on it. Moreover, those of us privileged to have choices about our work often choose a profession for its material benefits rather than its intrinsic value or its contribution to justice, which is one way work can be corrupting or "on the way to hell."

Although they approached the subject from different angles, Day and Peter Maurin shared a belief in the holiness of work and the need for work to be creative and humanizing. To this end, they advocated distributism, an economic theory (based on the principles of Catholic social teaching) that emphasizes wide ownership of property and local cooperatives, neither of which the striking miners enjoyed. Most of us do not work in anything like the grinding conditions of a coal mine, but most of us also do not think of our work in terms of holiness. Has your work been a testing ground? Think about the scope of God's providence and goodness in your work and the value it holds for your life.

Day Eighteen

Peter used to talk about a *philosophy of work and a philosophy of poverty.* Both are needed in order to change things as they are, to do away with the causes of war. The bravery to face voluntary poverty is needed if we wish to marry, to live, to produce children, to work for life instead of for death, to reject war.

A philosophy of work is essential if we would be whole men, holy men, healthy men, joyous men. A certain amount of goods is necessary for a man to lead a good life, and we have to make that kind of society where it is easier for men to be good. . . .

A philosophy of work and a philosophy of poverty are necessary if we would share with all men what we have, if we would each try to be the least, if we would wash the feet of our brothers. It is necessary if we would so choose to love our brother, live for him, and die for him, rather than kill him in war. We would need to reject the work in steel mills, mines, [and] factories which contributed to war. We would be willing to go on general strike, and we intend to keep talking about general strikes in order to familiarize each other, ourselves, [and] our fellow workers with the phrase, so that they will begin to ponder and try to understand what a different way of working, different jobs, a different attitude to work would mean in the lives of all.

Reflection

Not all of us are called to the degree of voluntary poverty that Day and Peter Maurin were, but all of us are called to get by with less and to remove ourselves as much as we can from the destructive aspects of our economy. Day believed that violence is not simply a consequence of anger or greed and cannot be prevented simply by convincing people to renounce it. Better working and living conditions make it easier for us to be peaceful and avoid conflict, and voluntary poverty fosters such conditions by removing people from industries that prioritize competition and consumption while grinding down those who make competition and consumption possible. For Day, a different attitude—choosing to sacrifice and choosing to think about work in its different forms—is an important part of sustaining peace. Ponder what comforts you could give up and what actions you could undertake in order to develop such an attitude.

It is not between good and evil, we repeat, that the choice lies, but between good and better. In other words, we must give up over and over again even the good things of this world to choose God. Mortal sin is a turning from God and a turning to created things—created things that are good.

It is so tremendous an idea that it is hard for people to see its implications. Our whole literature, our culture, is built on ethics, the choice between good and evil. The drama of the ages is on this theme. . . .

In all secular literature it has been so difficult to portray the good man, the saint, that a Don Quixote is a fool; the Prince Myshkin is an epileptic in order to arouse the sympathy of the reader, appalled by unrelieved goodness. There are, of course, the lives of the saints, but they are too often written as though they were not in this world. . . .

Too little has been stressed the idea that all are called. Too little attention has been placed on the idea of mass conversions. We have sinned against the virtue of hope. There have been in these days mass conversions to Nazism, fascism, and communism. Where are our saints to call the masses to God? Personalists first, we must put the question to ourselves. Communitarians, we will find Christ in our brothers.

Reflection

We rarely choose evil things knowing they are evil. Rather, we choose things we think are good for us. Our desire to love and be loved tempts us to choose things that are tangible and easily grasped. Most of these things are good in that they are created by God, but when we fail to acknowledge their source, we fail to see that they cannot satisfy our longings alone. Because we tend to treat ethics as a choice between obviously good or obviously evil things, we tend to think of ourselves as basically good for not having chosen the latter and to think of saints who gave up good things as having done something admirable but ultimately unnecessary. In a word, we are not as good as we think, and yet we are all called to be better. Consider the good things in your life—is there something you may be called to give up?

When Day was accused of being a communist or socialist, she would respond by calling herself a personalist. Personalism is a diverse philosophy that emphasizes the unique value of the human person; communitarianism is a philosophy that emphasizes the relationship between the individual and the community—specifically small, independent communities.

Day Twenty

The attributes of the soul are, according to St. Teresa, memory, understanding, and will. If you use these three, you can bring to life again your love for your husband, your memory of your first love for him, your understanding of his difficulties and the troubles that have come between you; your will to love him now. If only for self preservation you must use the will as you cannot go on in this state of unhappiness and friction. Love is a matter of the will anyway, when it isn't just a biological urge that beclouds every other issue. If you will to love someone (even the most repulsive and wicked), and try to serve him as an expression of that love,—then you soon come to *feel* love. And God will hear your prayers. "Enlarge Thou my heart that Thou mayest enter in!" You can pray the same way, that your heart may be enlarged to love again.

It is true that we cannot be happy unless we love, so it is worth making every effort to love. It is a question of deepest obligation for you since as a Catholic you have made this promise and you knew what you were doing. If your husband had been a Catholic these things would have come up too.

The union between man and woman is the closest analogy in this moral life to the union between God and man. One cannot properly be said to understand the love of God without understanding the deepest fleshly as well as spiritual love between man and woman. The two should go hand in hand. You cannot separate the soul from the body.

Reflection

One of the deepest needs experienced by human beings is our need to be loved. We experience this love spiritually in how we love and are loved by God but also in the ways we love other human beings. When we elevate the soul or spirit out of love for God, it should not mean rejecting the body. To her credit, Day does not do this, and as she notes in the next excerpt, she experienced a genuine, natural happiness with Batterham. At the same time, this happiness led her to long for a greater, supernatural happiness, for which she then gave up her relationship.

Day's honesty about her experiences is refreshing. We are created to love and cannot be happy unless we love, so we must learn to love in the right ways and for the right reasons. Reflect on your own experiences in these areas, praying that God will enlarge your heart and direct your love to its best ends.

This diary entry from 1937 indicates that Day continued to muse privately on what she called her common-law marriage with Forster Batterham a decade after she ended it by choosing to convert to Catholicism. She and Batterham were not in contact at the time, though years later they resumed a friendship.

In addition to referencing St. Teresa of Ávila's autobiography, Day quotes St. Augustine's *Confessions* ("Enlarge Thou my heart").

Day Twenty-One

One of the disconcerting facts about the spiritual life is that God takes you at your word. Sooner or later one is given a chance to prove his love. The very word "diligo," the Latin word used for "love," means "I prefer." It was all very well to love God in His works, in the beauty of His creation which was crowned for me by the birth of my child. Forster had made the physical world come alive for me and had awakened in my heart a flood of gratitude. The final object of this love and gratitude was God. No human creature could receive or contain so vast a flood of love and joy as I often felt after the birth of my child. With this came the need to worship, to adore. I had heard many say that they wanted to worship God in their own way and did not need a Church in which to praise Him, nor a body of people with whom to associate themselves. But I did not agree to this. My very experience as a radical, my whole make-up, led me to want to associate myself with others, with the masses, in loving and praising God. Without even looking into the claims of the Catholic Church, I was willing to admit that for me she was the one true Church.... It may have been an unthinking, unquestioning faith, and yet the chance certainly came, again and again, "Do I prefer the Church to my own will," even if it was only the small matter of sitting at home on a Sunday morning with the papers? And the choice was the Church.

Reflection

We may appreciate that God has given us free will, but we sometimes shrink from the responsibility it entails, particularly when it comes to the objects of our love. In Day's case, not only did she choose to leave a pleasurable, stable relationship with Batterham, she chose to join the Catholic Church, a decision seemingly incongruous with her radical background. Her faith remained firm, however, and God led her toward new communities in the church and with the people she cared for throughout her life. Day's conversion entailed giving up a relationship she valued, trusting God, and choosing the church over her own will. The choices we face are different than Day's, but we all experience moments where the choice we know to be right is not an easy choice to make. Reflect on a time when you made a difficult choice. What good did you gain from choosing to take the harder path?

This passage comes midway through *The Long Loneliness*, in a section Day titled "Natural Happiness" to describe the period in which she lived with Forster Batterham. During this period she occupied herself with reading, writing, getting to know their neighbors, and enjoying nature with Batterham, who loved to fish and garden. Still, her report of beginning to pray and attend Mass during this period indicates that her search for a different happiness was underway even before the birth of their daughter, Tamar.

Of course the church is corrupt! “But this corruption must put on incorruption,” St. Paul says, so I rejoice as I have in my short lifetime seen renewals going on, or read of them, and see the excitement, the joy of this sense of renewal. Certainly I knew when I became a Catholic that the church was a human institution and at first I had a sense of my betrayal of the working class, of the poor and oppressed for whom I had a romantic love and desire to serve. But just as I in my youth sought them out, lived in their slums and felt at home, so the Lord was seeking me out and I could not resist Him. And I found Him in the Church, in the Sacraments, life-giving and strength-giving, in spite of the American flag in the sanctuary, the boring sermons, the incomprehensible and mumbled Latin, the Sunday Catholic, the wide gulf between clergy and laity, even the contempt for the laity which I often felt, and even heard expressed, the down-grading of marriage by religious. . . .

How much criticism I could have written over the years of Church, priests, religious and laity too. They were a world apart from the life I had lived up thru my first 25 years.

But I read the lives of the saints, and knew that the renewal they brought—over and over, the St. Benedicts, St. Francis, St. Dominic, St. Vincent de Paul, St. Isaac Jogues, etc., etc., etc.—was not just a thing of the past but was going on, over and over.

Reflection

Many of us have had complaints about the church, whether the Catholic Church or another body, and some of us have had the same complaints Day recalls in this diary entry, written after she had been a Catholic for more than four decades.

One lesson that Day can teach us is that Christian faithfulness does not fit well anywhere on our political or religious spectrums. Like her readers, she sometimes had trouble reconciling her politics with her faith. Nevertheless, she looked for God in her chosen church even when doing so brought tension with that church or others who shared her political views. She honestly expresses her criticism, but she also finds signs of hope and renewal through saints she admires. Be on the lookout for renewal and other signs of God. While acknowledging human flaws and failures, where might you see hope for change?

The most significant thing about *The Catholic Worker* is poverty, some say.

The most significant thing is community, others say. We are not alone any more.

But the final word is love. At times it has been, in the words of Father Zossima, a harsh and dreadful thing, and our very faith in love has been tried through fire.

We cannot love God unless we love each other, and to love we must know each other. We know Him in the breaking of bread, and we know each other in the breaking of bread, and we are not alone any more. Heaven is a banquet and life is a banquet, too, even with a crust, where there is companionship.

We have all known the long loneliness and we have learned that the only solution is love and that love comes with community.

These lines are found in the postscript of Day's autobiography, although "the long loneliness" appears in several places in the text. She takes the phrase from a letter written by Mary Ward, an English nun who founded an order for women that paralleled the Jesuits even as she faced suppression by leaders in the Catholic Church.

Father Zossima is a character in Fyodor Dostoevsky's novel *The Brothers Karamazov*; he is a wise elder in the Orthodox Church.

Reflection

It can be difficult to love those closest to us, let alone strangers, especially in an age in which technology distances us from each other and makes us ever lonelier, but Day proposes that we start by eating together. In a later column she clarifies that although we experience loneliness, it is fundamentally a longing to return to God, the source of life. The good news is that we can begin to love God and experience community now by knowing and loving our fellow human beings. We can form community by joining together in "the breaking of the bread." Reach out and choose to share a meal with others, whether family, friends, or a new acquaintance, and as you eat, be aware of the community forming around you.

Another Catholic newspaper says it sympathizes with our sentimentality. This is a charge always leveled against pacifists. We are supposed to be afraid of the suffering, of the hardships of war.

But let those who talk of softness, of sentimentality, come to live with us in cold, unheated houses in the slums. . . . Let them live with rats, with vermin, bedbugs, roaches, lice. . . .

Let their flesh be mortified by cold, by dirt, by vermin; let their eyes be mortified by the sight of bodily excretions, diseased limbs, eyes, noses, mouths.

Let their noses be mortified by the smells of sewage, decay, and rotten flesh. . . .

Let their ears be mortified by harsh and screaming voices, by the constant coming and going of people living herded together with no privacy.

Let their taste be mortified by the constant eating of insufficient food cooked in huge quantities for hundreds of people, the coarser foods, so that there will be enough to go around; and the smell of such cooking is often foul.

Then when they have lived with these comrades, with these sights and sounds, let our critics talk of sentimentality. As we have often quoted Dostoevsky's Father Zossima, "Love in practice is a harsh and dreadful thing compared to love in dreams."

Reflection

If we doubt whether love in practice is, in fact, "a harsh and dreadful thing," even a small part of the way of life Day describes would convince us. Practicing love is never easy, and the sentimentality of our culture makes it even harder, as does the ability to take positions without cost. Whether or not one agrees with the Catholic Worker's pacifism, it is credible because Catholic Workers put it into practice. Choosing the hard reality of loving others over the ease of talking about our ideals is challenging but necessary. Consider what values and positions you hold dear and how you can actively live out your convictions despite the harsh realities that you might encounter.

Day Twenty-Five

We suffer these things and they fade from memory. But daily, hourly, to give up our own possessions and especially to subordinate our own impulses and wishes to others—these are hard, hard things; and I don't think they ever get any easier.

You can strip yourself, you can be stripped, but still you will reach out like an octopus to seek your own comfort, your untroubled time, your ease, your refreshment. It may mean books or music—the gratification of the inner senses—or it may mean food and drink, coffee and cigarettes. The one kind of giving up is no easier than the other.

Reflection

By and large, our culture encourages us to seek our own comfort (as if we needed much encouragement). Of the many consequences of being comfortable, the worst may be that it makes it seem normal for us to ignore the suffering of others. Life at a house of hospitality meant that Day could not ignore suffering; prior to this passage, she describes two unsettling encounters with women, one a beggar with cancer and another a drunken prostitute. As she occasionally admits, however, she enjoyed books, food, and so on partly because they allowed her to escape the daily grind of voluntary poverty. She understands that seeking comfort is a personal challenge, but she knows that it is one for all of us and that the greater challenge is not enduring what others do to us but overcoming our own selfish desires. Do you find it hard to subordinate your impulses and wishes to others? Give up something small today, with the goal of giving up something big soon.

Day Twenty-Six

People probably do not realize with what fear and trembling I speak or write about the Catholic Worker, our ideas and our point of view. It is an extreme point of view, and yet it is tested and proved over and over again; it is almost as if God says to us "Do you really mean what you say?" and then gives us a chance to prove it. We have to live with the positions we take, and at the same time we are bound to be beset with all kinds of human doubts: who are we, who have so seldom been tried and have not suffered as others have in war, to take such a position? . . . I know what human fear is and how often it keeps us from following our conscience. We find so many ways of rationalizing our positions.

Reflection

It is important to have a point of view and to take positions on significant issues. It is also important to test that point of view and to recognize that our positions are rarely, if ever, final. Day often boldly stated her positions, and she did mean what she said. Yet she was up-front about her doubts and concern that she had not done enough to support taking those positions. She shows us that it is possible to acknowledge complexity and incompleteness while seeking and proclaiming truth.

Testing our point of view should include listening to other people, considering other ideas, and returning to our own sources. This process may lessen our doubts, and it will certainly increase our understanding of and solidarity with our fellow human beings. Are there positions you have been unwilling to examine? Are there positions you have rationalized because they are safe? Find someone with whom you disagree to discuss your respective points of view.

Tradition! We scarcely know the word anymore. We are afraid to be either proud of our ancestors or ashamed of them. We scorn nobility in name and in fact. We cling to a bourgeois mediocrity which would make it appear we are all Americans, made in the image and likeness of George Washington, all of a pattern, all prospering if we are good, and going down in the world if we are bad.

Reflection

Our individualism means that we tend to be positive about tradition when it affirms our beliefs and practices and negative about it when it does not. Day touches on the subject while discussing immigrants, many of whom endure harsh working and living conditions and face pressure to conform to the customs and conventions of American society. The idea of discarding the past for the sake of freedom and opportunity has long been part of the American experience. Although this idea can bring people together, it also can lead people to cede the power and influence of their own traditions or ignore the value of traditions not their own. What do you appreciate about the tradition of your faith, family, or ethnic group? Where do you see value in other traditions?

There may be ever-improving standards of living in the United States, with every worker eventually owning his own home and driving his own car; but our whole modern economy is based on preparation for war, and this surely is one of the great arguments for poverty in our time. If the comfort one achieves results in the death of millions in the future, then that comfort shall be duly paid for. Indeed, to be literal, contributing to the war (misnamed "defense") effort is a very difficult to avoid. If you work in a textile mill making cloth, or in a factory making dungarees or blankets, your work is still tied up with war. If you raise food or irrigate the land to raise food, you may be feeding troops or liberating others to serve as troops. If you ride a bus you are paying taxes. Whatever you buy is taxed, so that you are, in effect, helping to support the state's preparations for war exactly to the extent of your attachment to worldly things of whatever kind.

The act and spirit of giving are the best counter to the evil forces in the world today, and giving liberates the individual not only spiritually but materially. For, in a world [of] enslavement through installment buying and mortgages, the only way to live in any true security is to live so close to the bottom that when you fall you do not have far to drop, you do not have much to lose.

Reflection

Regardless of how we perceive our economic and political systems, it is all but impossible to avoid involvement in them, and consequently we cannot simply wash our hands of their outcomes, good or bad. Day herself rode buses, but she also emphasized giving up the "worldly things" produced by her economy as well as being aware of the "enslavement" caused by the production and consumption of those things. The comfort of our possessions can create the illusion of security and blind us to the underside of our way of life. The less we cultivate the act and spirit of consumption and the more we cultivate those of giving, the better we will be able to assist those in need. How much do you think about your possessions and the cost of owning them, both for you and for others? Imagine more ways that you can give rather than receive.

Loaves and Fishes was published at the height of the Cold War (the year after the Cuban Missile Crisis) and in the midst of the postwar economic boom, which benefited Catholics as much as any group. Only two years earlier, however, President Dwight D. Eisenhower had used his farewell address to warn the nation of the rising "military-industrial complex."

We must prepare to fight for freedom here in America, they say, but we have lost our freedom here. People have come to accept the idea that we are a nation of industrial slaves, creatures of the State which doles out relief and jobs, and which is now going to seize the young and the strong for defense.

We have lost our democracy because we have lost our faith in men,—we no longer look upon them as creatures of body and soul, temples of the Holy Ghost, made to the image and likeness of God. If we have no faith in their spiritual capacities, we make no call on their spiritual resources.

Reflection

Our culture of consumerism creates the illusion of greater freedom by offering us an ever-widening selection of products and ever-increasing opportunities for entertainment and self-expression. As long as we buy more stuff and defend it with our lives, we will lose the ability to critically examine ourselves and our society. However, as soon as we recognize a higher claim on our bodies and souls, we will become less dependent on a powerful state, which is the heart of Day's critique of both capitalism and socialism. If we are going to discern the good and the bad of our government, we must learn to have faith in our "spiritual capacities" and call on our "spiritual resources." What capacities and resources do you possess? How might you direct them toward serving others?

People live, eat, sleep, love, worship, marry, have children, and somehow live in the midst of war, in the midst of anguish. The sun continues to shine, the leaves flaunt their vivid color, there is a serene warmth in the day and an invigorating cold at night.

Turn off your radio. Put away your daily paper. Read one review of events a week and spend some time reading such books as the above. They tell too of days of striving and of strife. They are of other centuries and also of our own. They make us realize that all times are perilous, that men live in a dangerous world, in peril constantly of losing or maiming soul and body.

We get some sense of perspective reading such books. Renewed courage and faith and even joy to live. And man cannot live long without joy, without some vestige of happiness to light up his days.

This excerpt is from a diary entry from September 1940, the same month the previous excerpt was published in the *Catholic Worker*. In the buildup to World War II, Day was under increasing pressure on account of her pacifist stand and recent testimony before Congress in opposition to conscription (the draft).

The books she refers to are novels by authors such as Graham Greene and Sigrid Undset along with the biblical books of Jeremiah and 1 Kings.

Reflection

Being conscious of the joy and beauty of everyday life, even "in the midst of anguish," is part of the little way of love that inspired Day throughout her half century at a house of hospitality. She had other inspirations, of course, including a lifelong love of literature that contributed to the sense of perspective she describes here. Finding joy in ordinary beauty and activities contributes to our ability to live in challenging times, but Day also suggests that reading reminds us that striving and strife have always been part of human life. This perspective—recognizing challenges human beings have faced across history—can give us renewed courage and, as Day says, even joy as we continue. Resolve to enrich your sense of perspective by reading something new as you finish this journey and begin the next.

Further Reading

Day, Dorothy. *Dorothy Day: Selected Writings*, edited by Robert Ellsberg. Maryknoll, NY: Orbis, 1992.

———. *Loaves and Fishes*. New York: Harper & Row, 1963.

———. *The Long Loneliness: The Autobiography of the Legendary Catholic Social Activist*. New York: Harper, 1952.

Forest, Jim. *All Is Grace: A Biography of Dorothy Day*. Rev. ed. Maryknoll, NY: Orbis, 2011.

Wright, Terrence C. *Dorothy Day: An Introduction to Her Life and Thought*. San Francisco: Ignatius Press, 2018.

Zwick, Mark, and Louise Zwick. *The Catholic Worker Movement: Intellectual and Spiritual Origins*. New York: Paulist, 2005.

Passages

Day 1: Dorothy Day, *From Union Square to Rome* (New York: Orbis, 2006), 166–67.

Day 2: Dorothy Day, "In Peace Is My Bitterness Most Bitter," *Catholic Worker*, January 1967.

Day 3: Dorothy Day, *All the Way to Heaven: The Selected Letters of Dorothy Day*, ed. Robert Ellsberg (New York: Image, 2010), 142.

Day 4: Dorothy Day, "Days with an End," *Catholic Worker*, April 1934.

Day 5: Dorothy Day, *House of Hospitality* (Huntington, IN: Our Sunday Visitor, 2015), 114.

Day 6: Dorothy Day, "Inventory," *Catholic Worker*, January 1951.

Day 7: Dorothy Day, "Are the Leaders Insane?," *Catholic Worker*, April 1954.

Day 8: Dorothy Day, *Loaves and Fishes* (New York: Harper & Row, 1963), 176

Day 9: Dorothy Day, *The Duty of Delight: The Diaries of Dorothy Day* (Milwaukee, WI: Marquette University Press, 2008), 351.

Day 10: Dorothy Day, *The Long Loneliness: The Autobiography of the Legendary Catholic Social Activist* (New York: Harper, 1952), 10–11.

Day 11: Day, *Loaves and Fishes*, 210.

Day 12: Day, *House of Hospitality*, 267.

Day 13: Dorothy Day, *On Pilgrimage* (Grand Rapids: Eerdmans, 2000), 123–24.

Day 14: Dorothy Day, *Writings from* Commonweal, ed. Patrick Jordan (Collegeville, MN: Liturgical Press, 2002), 101–2.

Day 15: Dorothy Day, "The Use of Force," *Catholic Worker*, November 1936.

Day 16: Dorothy Day, "Explains CW Stand on Use Use of Force," *Catholic Worker*, September 1938.

Day 17: Dorothy Day, "Reflections on Work," *Catholic Worker*, December 1946.

Day 18: Day, *On Pilgrimage*, 151–52.

Day 19: Day, *On Pilgrimage*, 162–63.

Day 20: Day, *Duty of Delight*, 29.

Day 21: Day, *Long Loneliness*, 139.

Day 22: Day, *Duty of Delight*, 484.

Day 23: Day, *Long Loneliness*, 285–86.

Day 24: Dorothy Day, "Why Do the Members of Christ Tear One Another?," *Catholic Worker*, February 1942.

Day 25: Day, *Loaves and Fishes*, 84.

Day 26: Dorothy Day, "Fear in Our Time," *Catholic Worker*, April 1968.

Day 27: Day, *Long Loneliness*, 16.

Day 28: Day, *Loaves and Fishes*, 86.

Day 29: Dorothy Day, "Wars Are Caused by Man's Loss of His Faith in Man," *Catholic Worker*, September 1940.

Day 30: Day, *Duty of Delight*, 65.